FRANCIS FRITH'

NEWARK PHOTOC
MEMORIE

THE FRANCIS FRITH COLLECTION

www.francisfrith.com

PHOTOGRAPHIC MEMORIES

Francis Frith's
AROUND NEWARK-ON-TRENT

Clive Hardy

First published in the United Kingdom in 2000 by
The Francis Frith Collection

British Library Cataloguing in Publication Data

Around Newark-on-Trent
Clive Hardy
ISBN 1-85937-366-6

The Francis Frith Collection
Frith's Barn, Teffont,
Salisbury, Wiltshire SP3 5QP
Tel: +44 (0) 1722 716 376
Email: info@francisfrith.co.uk
www.francisfrith.com

Printed and bound in Great Britain

Front Cover: Bridge Street 1906 56492t

The colour-tinting is for illustrative purposes only, and is not intended to be historically accurate

AS WITH ANY HISTORICAL DATABASE THE FRITH ARCHIVE IS CONSTANTLY BEING CORRECTED AND IMPROVED AND THE PUBLISHERS WOULD WELCOME INFORMATION ON OMISSIONS OR INACCURACIES

Contents

FRANCIS FRITH: *Victorian Pioneer*

FRANCIS FRITH, Victorian founder of the world-famous photographic archive, was a complex and multitudinous man. A devout Quaker and a highly successful Victorian businessman, he was both philosophic by nature and pioneering in outlook.

By 1855 Francis Frith had already established a wholesale grocery business in Liverpool, and sold it for the astonishing sum of £200,000, which is the equivalent today of over £15,000,000. Now a multi-millionaire, he was able to indulge his passion for travel. As a child he had pored over travel books written by early explorers, and his fancy and imagination had been stirred by family holidays to the sublime mountain regions of Wales and Scotland. 'What a land of spirit-stirring and enriching scenes and places!' he had written. He was to return to these scenes of grandeur in later years to 'recapture the thousands of vivid and tender memories', but with a different purpose. Now in his thirties, and captivated by the new science of photography, Frith set out on a series of pioneering journeys to the Nile regions that occupied him from 1856 until 1860.

INTRIGUE AND ADVENTURE

He took with him on his travels a specially-designed wicker carriage that acted as both dark-room and sleeping chamber. These far-flung journeys were packed with intrigue and adventure. In his life story, written when he was sixty-three, Frith tells of being held captive by bandits, and of fighting 'an awful midnight battle to the very point of surrender with a deadly pack of hungry, wild dogs'. Sporting flowing Arab costume, Frith arrived at Akaba by camel seventy years before Lawrence, where he encountered 'desert princes and rival sheikhs, blazing with jewel-hilted swords'.

During these extraordinary adventures he was assiduously exploring the desert regions bordering the Nile and patiently recording the antiquities and peoples with his camera. He was the first photographer to venture beyond the sixth cataract. Africa was still the mysterious 'Dark Continent', and Stanley and Livingstone's historic meeting was a decade into the future. The conditions for picture taking confound belief. He laboured for hours in his wicker darkroom in the sweltering heat of the desert, while the volatile chemicals fizzed dangerously in their trays. Often he was forced to work in remote tombs and caves where conditions were cooler. Back in London he exhibited his photographs and was 'rapturously cheered' by members of the Royal Society. His reputation as a photographer was made overnight. An eminent modern historian has likened their impact on the population of the time to that on our own generation of the first photographs taken on the surface of the moon.

Venture of a Life-Time

Characteristically, Frith quickly spotted the opportunity to create a new business as a specialist publisher of photographs. He lived in an era of immense and sometimes violent change. For the poor in the early part of Victoria's reign work was a drudge and the hours long, and people had precious little free time to enjoy themselves.

Most had no transport other than a cart or gig at their disposal, and had not travelled far beyond the boundaries of their own town or village. However, by the 1870s, the railways had threaded their way across the country, and Bank Holidays and half-day Saturdays had been made obligatory by Act of Parliament. All of a sudden the ordinary working man and his family were able to enjoy days out and see a little more of the world.

With characteristic business acumen, Francis Frith foresaw that these new tourists would enjoy having souvenirs to commemorate their days out. In 1860 he married Mary Ann Rosling and set out with the intention of photographing every city, town and village in Britain. For the next thirty years he travelled the country by train and by pony and trap, producing fine photographs of seaside resorts and beauty spots that were keenly bought by millions of Victorians. These prints were painstakingly pasted into family albums and pored over during the dark nights of winter, rekindling precious memories of summer excursions.

The Rise of Frith & Co

Frith's studio was soon supplying retail shops all over the country. To meet the demand he gathered about him a small team of photographers, and published the work of independent artist-photographers of the calibre of Roger Fenton and Francis Bedford. In order to gain some understanding of the scale of Frith's business one only has to look at the catalogue issued by Frith & Co in 1886: it runs to some 670

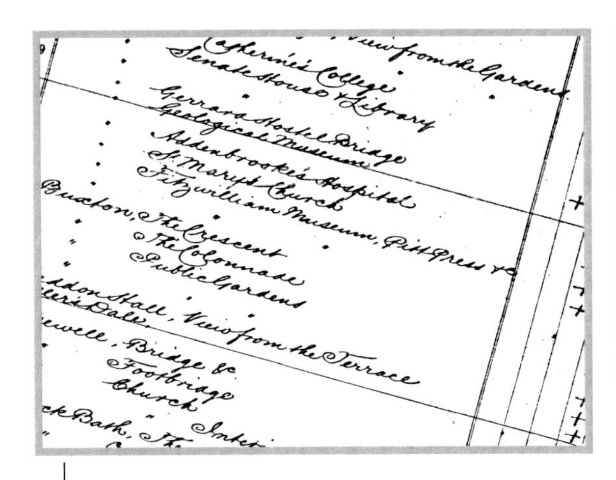

Catherine's College, View from the Garden
Senate House & Library
Gerrard Hostel Bridge
Geological Museum
Addenbrooke's Hospital
St. Mary's Church
Fitzwilliam Museum, Pitt Press &c
Buxton, The Crescent
" The Colonnade
" Public Gardens
ddon Hall, View from the Terrace
well, Bridge &c
" Footbridge
" Church
ck Bath, " Inter

pages, listing not only many thousands of views of the British Isles but also many photographs of most European countries, and China, Japan, the USA and Canada – note the sample page shown above from the hand-written *Frith & Co* ledgers detailing pictures taken. By 1890 Frith had created the greatest specialist photographic publishing company in the world, with over 2,000 outlets – more than the combined number that Boots and WH Smith have today! The picture on the right shows the *Frith & Co* display board at Ingleton in the Yorkshire Dales. Beautifully constructed with mahogany frame and gilt inserts, it could display up to a dozen local scenes.

Postcard Bonanza

The ever-popular holiday postcard we know today took many years to develop. In 1870 the Post Office issued the first plain cards, with a pre-printed stamp on one face. In 1894 they allowed other publishers' cards to be sent through the mail with an attached adhesive halfpenny stamp. Demand grew rapidly, and in 1895 a new size of postcard was permitted called the court card, but there was little room for illustration. In 1899, a year after Frith's death, a new card measuring 5.5 x 3.5 inches became the standard format, but it was not until 1902 that the divided back came into being, with address and message on one face and a full-size illustration on the other. *Frith & Co* were in the vanguard of postcard development, and Frith's sons Eustace and Cyril continued their father's monumental task, expanding the number of views offered to the public and recording more and more places in Britain, as the coasts and countryside were opened up to mass travel.

Francis Frith died in 1898 at his villa in Cannes, his great project still growing. The archive he created continued in business for another seventy years. By 1970 it contained over a third of a million pictures of 7,000 cities, towns and villages. The massive photographic record Frith has left to us stands as a living monument to a special and very remarkable man.

Frith's Archive: *A Unique Legacy*

Francis Frith's legacy to us today is of immense significance and value, for the magnificent archive of evocative photographs he created provides a unique record of change in 7,000 cities, towns and villages throughout Britain over a century and more. Frith and his fellow studio photographers revisited locations many times down the years to update their views, compiling for us an enthralling and colourful pageant of British life and character.

We tend to think of Frith's sepia views of Britain as nostalgic, for most of us use them to conjure up memories of places in our own lives with which we have family associations. It often makes us forget that to Francis Frith they were records of daily life as it was actually being lived in the cities, towns and villages of his day. The Victorian age was one of great and often bewildering change for ordinary people, and though the pictures evoke an impression of slower times, life was as busy and hectic as it is today.

We are fortunate that Frith was a photographer of the people, dedicated to recording the minutiae of everyday life. For it is this sheer wealth of visual data, the painstaking chronicle of changes in dress, transport, street layouts, buildings, housing, engineering and landscape that captivates us so much today. His remarkable images offer us a powerful link with the past and with the lives of our ancestors.

See Frith at www. frithbook.com

Today's Technology

Computers have now made it possible for Frith's many thousands of images to be accessed almost instantly. In the Frith archive today, each photograph is carefully 'digitised' then stored on a CD Rom. Frith archivists can locate a single photograph amongst thousands within seconds. Views can be catalogued and sorted under a variety of categories of place and content to the immediate benefit of researchers. Inexpensive reference prints can be created for them at the touch of a mouse button, and a wide range of books and other printed materials assembled and published for a wider, more general readership - in the next twelve months over a hundred Frith local history titles will be published!

The day-to-day workings of the archive are very different from how they were in Francis Frith's time: imagine the herculean task of sorting through eleven tons of glass negatives as Frith had to do to locate a particular sequence of pictures! Yet the archive still prides itself on maintaining the same high standards of excellence laid down by Francis Frith, including the painstaking cataloguing and indexing of every view.

It is curious to reflect on how the internet now allows researchers in America and elsewhere greater instant access to the archive than Frith himself ever enjoyed. Many thousands of individual views can be called up on screen within seconds on one of the Frith internet sites, enabling people living continents away to revisit the streets of their ancestral home town, or view places in Britain where they have enjoyed holidays. Many overseas researchers welcome the chance to view special theme selections, such as transport, sports, costume and ancient monuments.

We are certain that Francis Frith would have heartily approved of these modern developments, for he himself was always working at the very limits of Victorian photographic technology.

The Value of the Archive Today

Because of the benefits brought by the computer, Frith's images are increasingly studied by social historians, by researchers into genealogy and ancestory, by architects, town planners, and by teachers and schoolchildren involved in local history projects. In addition, the archive offers every one of us a unique opportunity to examine the places where we and our families have lived and worked down the years. Immensely successful in Frith's own era, the archive is now, a century and more on, entering a new phase of popularity.

The Past in Tune with the Future

Historians consider the Francis Frith Collection to be of prime national importance. It is the only archive of its kind remaining in private ownership and has been valued at a million pounds. However, this figure is now rapidly increasing as digital technology enables more and more people around the world to enjoy its benefits.

Francis Frith's archive is now housed in an historic timber barn in the beautiful village of Teffont in Wiltshire. Its founder would not recognize the archive office as it is today. In place of the many thousands of dusty boxes containing glass plate negatives and an all-pervading odour of photographic chemicals, there are now ranks of computer screens. He would be amazed to watch his images travelling round the world at unimaginable speeds through network and internet lines.

The archive's future is both bright and exciting. Francis Frith, with his unshakeable belief in making photographs available to the greatest number of people, would undoubtedly approve of what is being done today with his lifetime's work. His photographs, depicting our shared past, are now bringing pleasure and enlightenment to millions around the world a century and

NEWARK-ON-TRENT – *An Introduction*

IT IS NOT certain when the area we now know as Newark was first inhabited, but an Anglo-Saxon burial site at Millgate dates from the early 5th century, and during the late 8th and early 9th centuries Newark formed one of the eight wapentakes of the 'army' of Nottingham - one of the Five Boroughs of the Danelaw. Here Danish law and customs held sway: the Scandinavians voted at public meetings literally with a show of weapons - today we just raise an arm. Just when the lands of the 'army' of Nottingham became Nottinghamshire is unclear, but it was probably around AD920, following the conquest of the Danelaw south of the Humber by the combined forces of Edward the Elder of Wessex and his sister Aethelflaed of Mercia.

It was under Alexander, Bishop of Lincoln, that Newark began to prosper; for much of the medieval period not only was it a similar size to Nottingham, it was also its main commercial rival. During the reign of Edward III, Flemish weavers and merchants were encouraged to settle in the town, which had become a leading export centre for wool bound for the Low Countries.

Straddling the Fosse Way and the road to York, Newark was one of only a handful of places where the Trent was bridged, so possession of the town, and more importantly its castle, could be of strategic significance. Today Newark Castle is just a splendid ruin, but it has played its part in the often turbulent history of England. It was Alexander, Bishop of Lincoln and lord of the manor, who replaced the original Norman timber fortress with one of stone, employing Ranulph of Durham to build the gatehouse; the end result was that Newark was one of the finest castles in 12th-century England.

In 1199 John, the youngest son of Henry II, finally succeeded to the throne following the death of his brother Richard the Lionheart. John proved to be an unpopular monarch: his reign, which was characterised by high taxation at home and the loss of vast territories, including Normandy to the French, led him into conflict with many of his barons. On top of this, John's relationship with the Catholic Church could at best be described as fraught. He strongly believed that the Church had no business sticking its nose into matters of State, and his clashes with the Papal Legate and the Pope were contributory factors leading to him being excommunicated.

By 1216 the country was in a state of civil war, and October of that year found the King at the Cistercian abbey of Swineshead near Boston. We know that John died at Newark Castle; what we are not sure about is how. One theory is that is was from over-eating, another is that it was from dysentery; and there are two traditions involving Swineshead Abbey, a monk named Simon and poison. Intending to murder the King, Simon sought absolution from his abbot, saying 'I am contented to lose my life, and so become a martyr, that I may utterly destroy this tyrant'. Simon then went into the abbey gardens, found a large toad, and extracted its poison. He mixed the poison into a cup of wine which he offered to the king, saying 'If it shall like your princely majesty, here is a cup of wine as ye never drank better before in all your lifetime; I trust this wassail shall make all England glad'. Whilst the King drank, Simon went to the farmary and committed suicide, probably by drinking neat some of the poison he had taken from the toad.

John was soon feeling extremely ill; suspecting the worst, he ordered Simon to be brought before him. On being told that Simon was already dead, the King was taken by carriage to Sleaford Castle; he was already too ill to ride his horse. From Sleaford he was brought to Newark, where he died on 19th October. His body was embalmed and taken to Worcester, where it was buried. His entrails were interred at Croxton Abbey. In the other story involving Swineshead, John is said to have been poisoned because he was lusting after the Abbot's sister. In this tradition he was given poisoned pears to eat.

There is also another variation to the story, that John survived long enough for his son, the nine-year-old Prince Henry, to be brought to Newark, where he proclaimed him his successor. It was not an automatic succession, for there were many who wanted Prince Louis of France to be proclaimed; but Prince Henry

had a champion in William, the earl marschal, who persuaded many barons to change sides. By the end of September 1217 the French had been forced to come to terms, and Henry III's throne was secure.

Newark's golden age was during the Middle Ages, when it was a serious rival to Nottingham. The town grew rich on sheep and wool, especially during the reign of Edward III, who actively encouraged Flemish weavers and merchants to settle in England. Flemish immigration and the introduction of the spinning wheel into more rural areas were both factors in the significant increase in cloth woven in England. From Newark wool and cloth were exported to the Low Countries by way of Boston and Hull. Wool continued to play an important role in the commercial success of Newark, but there were other industries such as tanning, brewing and milling.

Like all towns, Newark had its fair share of poor people. During the reign of James I an act was introduced whereby a House of Correction should be established in every shire 'to set idle persons to work'. The governor was empowered to set rogues to work at spinning and weaving haircloth and sackcloth, spinning Jersey woollen or linen yarn, and to punish them for any wrongdoing 'by putting fetters or gives upon them, and by a moderate whipping of them'. Newark had a whipping post. During the mid 17th century, the local House of Correction appears to have been at Southwell, but governor Samuel Thompson, who was into any number of business opportunities, took it upon himself to relocate the institution to Newark. An entry dated 3 April 1654, in which Thompson is effectively given the sack, states that 'he hath neglected his other employment. Ordered that another person be master of the Correction house'. Newark also had a pillory, one of only a handful known of in Nottinghamshire. A typical sentence was the one given to William Key: he was pilloried on 12 July 1692 for three hours and ordered to pay 10s compensation to Samuel and Thomas Martin.

By the Sword Divided

During the Civil War, Newark was destined to play a significant role in the King's cause by becoming a prominent Royalist stronghold. In December 1642 the Parliamentarian forces of Derbyshire, Nottinghamshire, Leicestershire, Lincolnshire, Rutland, Northamptonshire, Bedfordshire, Buckinghamshire and Huntingdonshire were brought together under the East Midlands Association. Among the Association's aims and objectives were plans to combine their forces so as to meet any Royalist threat within their area, and to put the Royalist garrisons in their counties under siege. In February 1643 an Association force, made up of troops from Derbyshire, Nottinghamshire and Lincolnshire, attempted to besiege Newark, which was heavily fortified with earthworks and artillery emplacements; however, they failed to make any impression and eventually withdrew.

Skirmishes between the Nottingham and Newark garrisons were a regular feature of the war. In September 1643 Royalists from Newark mounted a daring raid on Nottingham; they were allegedly aided by Royalist sympathiser Alderman Francis Toplady, who happened to command Nottingham's night guard, and is said to have let them in through one of the town gates. The Royalists quickly established a strong point in St Nicholas' Church, which they held for several days. As the steeple overlooked the castle grounds, the Royalists were well placed to engage in a little sniping. It took time to dislodge the raiders, who returned to Newark with a prisoner, mayor Richard Hardmett. As a result of the raid the garrison commander, 28-year-old Colonel Hutchinson, was convinced that he could not hold both the town and the castle with the forces available to him. He decided to hold the castle, and ordered the artillery on the town's ramparts to be withdrawn there; to stop any further sniping, St Nicholas's was ordered to be demolished. In April 1645 a raiding force from Newark captured one of Nottingham's outer defensive positions, a fort on Trent Bridge, which they held for two months.

In early 1644 Newark was once again under siege, this time by Sir John Meldrum with 5000 foot and 2000 horse. Sir John made a determined effort to take Newark, but was forced to call off the enterprise when his horse were routed by Prince Rupert. A brilliant if often reckless field commander, Prince Rupert made full use of Meldrum's plight by going on and capturing Lincoln.

On 7 May 1645 the King, accompanied by Prince Rupert and Prince Maurice, led a royal army of about 11,000 men out of Oxford. The King's field commanders were divided as to the most favourable course of action: Rupert was for heading north-west to relieve the besieged garrison at Chester, or to link up with James Graham, Marquis of Montrose, whose ragtag army of Highlanders and Irish had won numerous victories even when heavily outnumbered. Other commanders were for heading into the West Country to seek out and neutralise, or even better destroy, Sir Thomas Fairfax's army. In the end Charles compromised: Goring was sent west to confront Fairfax, while the King moved north with the main body of the army.

Unfortunately, events were to move somewhat quicker than the King's army. At Market Drayton, Charles learned that far from being in the West Country, Fairfax was besieging Oxford, and that Sir William Brereton had lifted his siege of Chester. Taking Rupert's advice, the King turned east to attack Leicester; it fell in less than one hour, and offered the Royalists a base for operations into East Anglia. Charles then moved to relieve Oxford, but before doing so allowed part of his cavalry to return to Newark. The fall of Leicester, however, had forced Fairfax to lift the siege of Oxford and move north; while the King was hunting near Daventry, he was told that Fairfax was only a few miles away. Charles had two options: he could fall back on Leicester, or he could fight. Rupert advised withdrawal, but the King, backed by Digby and Ashburnham, gave the orders for the army to move on to the obscure Northamptonshire village of Naseby, where he intended to fight. Though the Royalists were heavily outnumbered, Naseby was the last major battle of the Civil War in which the King still had a chance of victory, especially if Rupert could pull some of his unorthodox and highly effective cavalry tactics out of the bag.

Following his defeat at Naseby, the fall of Bristol was the next serious blow to the King's cause. Prince Rupert had again taken command of the 2000-strong garrison; but after touring the defences, his assessment was that it was impossible to hold - a militarily correct evaluation. Rupert's problems were compounded by an outbreak of plague and the suspect loyalty of many Bristolians, who had been given assurances by Fairfax and Cromwell that safety of their persons and property was guaranteed if they would surrender. The final assault began on 10 September and was over within a few hours. Rupert and his men were granted terms and

allowed to leave. Bristol's loss not only robbed the Royalists of a much needed port, but it also undermined the King's credibility with those foreign powers who might offer him assistance in the form of money, munitions or troops.

Charles was left with few options. He could strike north and attempt a link with Montrose, or he could seek a battle with the main Parliamentarian field army and hope to destroy it. He chose the former, and headed north-west, entering Chester on 23 September. The following day Charles watched from the Phoenix Tower on the city wall as Sir Marmaduke Langdale led the Royalist army out to do battle against the Parliamentarians on Rowton Heath. At best the battle could be described as chaotic; the outcome was that the last Royalist field army of any substance was effectively destroyed. On 25 September the king left Chester and headed west, then east towards Newark, now the only major Royalist garrison in the north. Three days later at Denbigh Charles heard that his last hope, Montrose, had been defeated at Philiphaugh.

The King reached Newark on 4 October. He made a foray as far as Welbeck, but was back in Newark by the time Prince Rupert arrived, demanding that the Council of War judge his actions in surrendering Bristol. Charles agreed; on the 21st he accepted the court's findings that whilst Rupert could have held out a few days longer, he was not guilty of lacking courage, or of betraying his King. Rupert's break with the King came a few days later when Sir Richard Willis, governor of Newark, was replaced by Lord Bellasis. Rupert, supported by Maurice and Gerard, demanded that Sir Richard be reinstated. There was a heated exchange which is said to have verged on mutiny: this resulted in Rupert and his followers leaving Newark on the 28th.

It was at Oxford in April 1646 that Charles finally made up his mind to surrender to the Scottish force taking part in the siege of Newark. On 5 May he surrendered in person to the Scots, who were astounded to see him; they immediately opened negotiations with the English Parliamentarians to sell the king to them. The following day, terms were agreed, and Newark surrendered on the king's orders. Even before its surrender, Parliament had taken the decision to slight Newark's fortifications and make the castle untenable. On 1 March 1647 Parliament issued instructions for its garrison to be withdrawn and slighting to begin. When Celia Fiennes visited Newark in the 1690s, she wrote that it was 'demolished so that only the ruinated walls remain'. Slighting was, however, carried out in varying degrees: Nottingham Castle was all but destroyed, but at Newark the three-storey gatehouse, three towers and the curtain survived.

After the Civil War the widows of Parliamentarian soldiers and former soldiers too badly wounded to earn a living could apply for a pension, but it was not until after the Restoration that former Royalist soldiers or their widows received the same relief. In January 1661 Jo Dingle and Richard Pearson, former members of the Newark garrison, were awarded pensions of forty shillings a year. As late as the 1690s pensions were still being awarded to former members of the Newark garrison, though from 1681 the amounts they received were reduced by half.

TRENT BRIDGE c1955 N12053

For centuries, the repair of bridges and maintenance of roads was the responsibility of the parishes in which they were situated, though important crossing points were often maintained through a levy raised from a number of parishes. Between 1678 and 1695 the parish of Kelham was indicted on numerous occasions for failing to repair 'a footbridge situate near the eastern end of Tunebridge, and leading from Muskham to Newark, a market town'. Newark itself was indicted on more than one occasion for failing to maintain bridges.

TRENT BRIDGE c1955 N12052

Newark owes much of its development to the fact that Henry I gave Alexander, Bishop of Lincoln, permission to divert the route of the Fosse Way through the town. In the late 17th century the main road from Nottingham to Newark went via Charlton (Carlton), Burton, Gunthorp (Gunthorpe), Horingham Ferry (Hoveringham), Bleasby Ferry and Stoak (Stoke) where it joined the Fosse Way.

Trent Bridge 1900 45104

This view shows Trent Bridge with the Ossington on the left, the castle on the right and the spire of St Mary Magdalen in the background. One interesting fact about St Mary's is that the 252ft-high spire is thirty feet longer than the ground plan of the main body of the building.

Ossington Coffee Palace 1890 24659

Erected in 1882 as a coffee house and temperance hotel by Viscountess Ossington as a memorial to her late husband. The Palace is said to be a replica of a 17th-century hostelry. For those wishing to partake of Warwick & Sons' ales and stouts, the George & Dragon is but a stagger away.

FROM TRENT BRIDGE 1909 61796
In those relatively traffic-free days before the Great War, it was still common practice for pedestrians to use the carriageway as an extension of the pavement. Judging from the angle of the picture, traffic was light enough for our cameraman to position his plate camera and tripod in the roadway.

FROM TRENT BRIDGE c1965 N12080
It is worth comparing this picture with the previous one. How many differences can you make out? For a start, two of the buildings in the background are no longer imposing town houses; one is now the offices of the Phoenix Assurance Co, and the other, Warwick house and former home of brewer Samuel Sketchley, has been converted into the Castle Garage.

GREAT NORTH ROAD c1955 N12007
This picture was taken for possible use as a postcard. In those days the Frith cameraman would be under instructions not to take the picture until the view was relatively free of traffic and pedestrians. The reason was purely commercial: Frith always attempted to get maximum mileage out of their postcards, and did not want anything in the picture that might date it too quickly.

TOWN LOCK c1965 N12090

Town Lock is one of two mechanised locks; the other is Newark Nether Lock at the northern end of the branch. To the right can be seen a part of the old hand-operated lock, which was eventually partially roofed for use as a drydock.

TOWN LOCK c1965 N12108A

By the side of Town Lock is this heavily-buttressed building. It looks as if a part of the original structure was demolished to make way for the canal, and the quadrant window fitted as an afterthought. It was once a pub, and no doubt a haunt of many a bargee.

THE CASTLE C1965 N12081
Despite its slighting, Newark Castle is still imposing. To the left is the splendid three-storey gatehouse built by the cathedral masons of Alexander, Bishop of Lincoln. Nearest the camera is the north-west tower, hexagonal in design, and to its right is the postern gate.

THE CASTLE CRYPT 1904 51735
The crypt, as it is called, is a vaulted apartment located in the northern part of the west front. It is 45ft long by 22ft wide, and its outer wall is 7ft 6in thick. Though it looks Norman, it is 13th-century; given the then layout of the castle, it was almost certainly used as a guardroom.

THE CASTLE AND THE GARDENS 1904 51732
The oldest picture we have that is taken from this angle is dated 1890; the only difference is that in those days the gatehouse was ivy-free. The gatehouse, 45 ft by 30 ft with walls nine feet thick, was designed and built by Ranulph of Durham, and is one of the earliest examples of a gatehouse fulfilling the role of a keep.

THE CASTLE AND THE FOOTBRIDGE 1890 24648
As can be seen here, the river formed part of the castle's defences. The landward defences included a moat, a drawbridge and a barbican. During the English Civil War the castle was the focal point of the town's defences, but there were other extensive fortifications including the Queen's Sconce, a star-shaped artillery emplacement, and one of the most impressive Civil War fortifications to survive to this day. Covering three acres, it controlled the point where the Fosse Way crossed the River Devon. The wooden bridge was built in 1827 to take the canal towpath over to millrace.

The Castle and the Free Library 1895 35549

The library was paid for by Sir William Gilstrap (1816-1896) who had made his money as a maltster. He also contributed to the fund that enabled the castle grounds to be converted from a cattle market to public gardens.

Castle Gate 1904 51741

This view looks down Castle Gate and the road to Leicester and Nottingham. In later years the house on the extreme left of the picture would become the Castle Garage. The marooned ornate street lamp would end its days painted with black and white bands and carrying signposts for London, Grantham, Leicester, Nottingham, Sleaford, Gainsborough and Lincoln. On the left is the Ram Hotel, once one of Newarks principal coaching inns.

FREEMAN, HARDY & WILLIS LTD

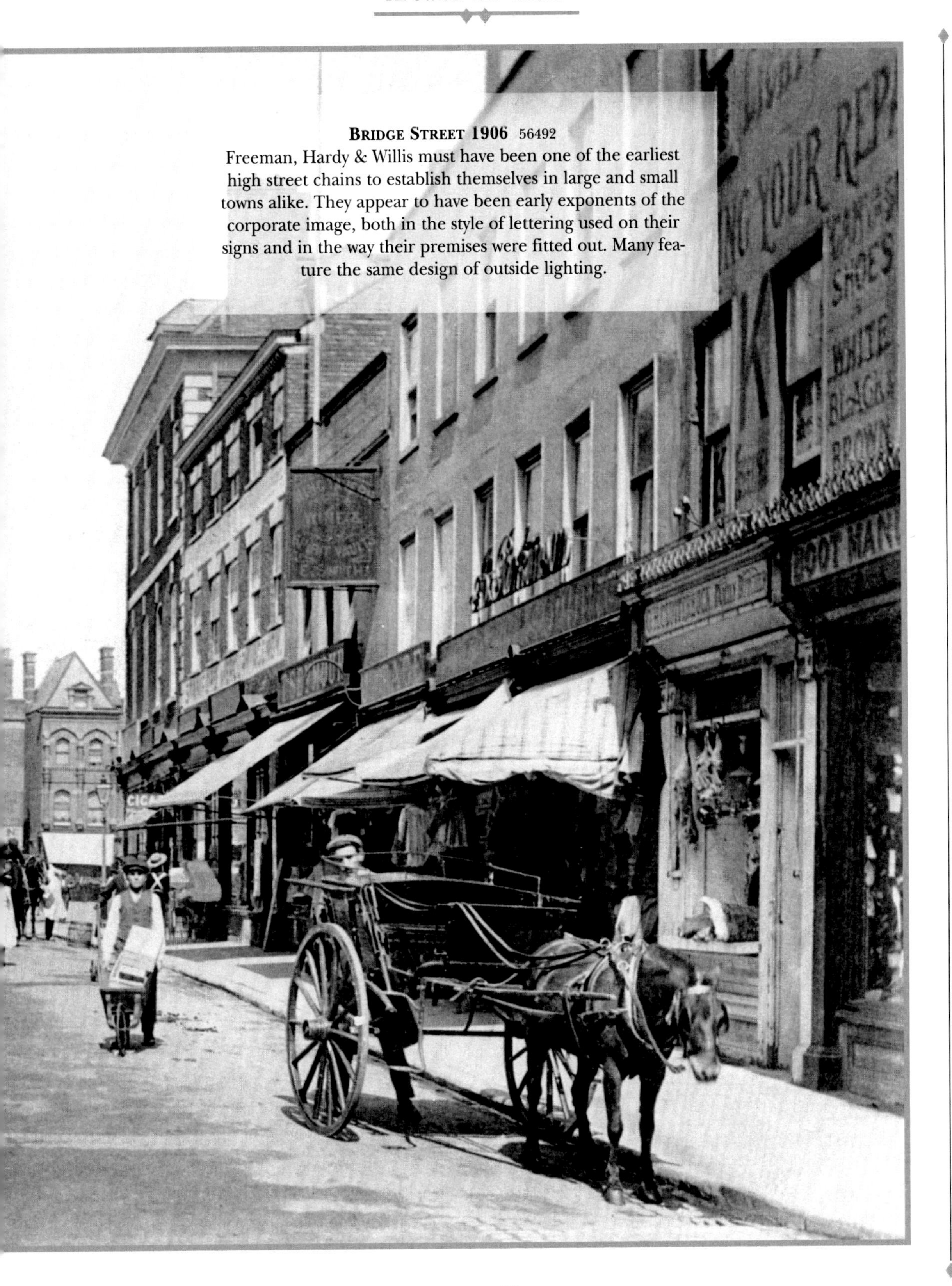

Bridge Street 1906 56492
Freeman, Hardy & Willis must have been one of the earliest high street chains to establish themselves in large and small towns alike. They appear to have been early exponents of the corporate image, both in the style of lettering used on their signs and in the way their premises were fitted out. Many feature the same design of outside lighting.

Stodman Street 1906 56494

Sunlight and shadow in Stodman Street. On the left the butcher takes time out for a chat, while the young boys are either intrigued by the antics of our cameraman, or waiting for something to run him over. The butcher's shop is interesting in that it is open on two sides; the butcher either cuts his meat in the street, or he has brought the block out to swill it down.

GOVERNOR'S OLD HOUSE 1909 61804

Situated in Stodman Street, this is where Prince Rupert had his quarters. It was the replacement of Governor Sir Richard Willis by Lord Bellasis that is said to have led to the final split between Rupert and King Charles.

GOVERNOR'S HOUSE, STODMAN STREET c1955 N12037
J Graham are offering better furniture on cash or terms (the never-never?), while at J C Stanger flour was around 1s 3d for a 3lb bag; butter 2s 6d a pound; and eggs 3s 10d a dozen.

THE FREE LIBRARY 1890 24661
As well as this library, paid for by Sir William Gilstrap, there was also the Newark Stock Library, whose honorary librarian in 1854 was Richard Sketchley, who worked for 'Punch' magazine. The library needed funds, so Sketchley approached the South Kensington Museum and persuaded them to lend various bits and pieces for an exhibition. Sketchley was later appointed assistant keeper of the Science & Art Department of the Victoria & Albert Museum.

WINE
AND
SPIRIT
MERCHANTS
ALE
FRYS CHOCOLATE
NEWARK

Appleton Gate 1906 56498

A cart horse of Dickens & Co, brewers and wine and spirits merchants, waits patiently between trips. Lighter loads were taken around town by handcart. It was on this street that a chantry house was provided, built by the widow of wealthy Newark merchant Alan Flemyng. Chantry priests were not usually a part of the establishment of a church or cathedral; they were independent. The function of a chantry priest was to say a mass every day for the soul of some departed citizen, the costs having been provided for in the dead person's estate, often in the form of rents from property.

APPLETON GATE 1909 61797
Note the large gilt letters above Bradford House. This was one of the principal ways in which Victorian and Edwardian retailers advertised the location of their premises; on large city stores the letters were often six feet high. With the advent of electric lighting, adventurous retailers had their signs modified to take lightbulbs so that they could be lit up after dark.

KIRK'S
PURE SWEETS
BRADFORD HOUSE
THE
BRADFORD
STUFF
HOUSE

APPLETON GATE c1955 N12030
In the General Election, the Conservatives were returned for a second term with an increased majority, despite the fact that the country had been hit by a wave of strikes. Income tax was reduced by a massive 6d in the pound, the second such cut since 1953; this probably gave the young mothers in our picture a few extra shillings a week in their housekeeping allowance.

MARKET PLACE 1904 51736
The Palladian-style Town Hall designed by John Carr dominates the background. Carr was one of the great architects of the late 18th century; his work includes the most important buildings in the former spa resort of Buxton, Derbyshire. Both the Crescent (built 1780-84) and the Great Stables (built 1789) were designed by Carr for the fifth Duke of Devonshire; the Great Stables are somewhat better known in their present guise as the Royal Devonshire Hospital.

THE TOWN HALL c1955
During the 18th century the combined surplus income from a number of local charities was sufficient to enable the Corporation to embark on a redevelopment programme that included the building of a new town jail, a workhouse, and a new Town Hall. There were sufficient funds to enable Carr to design a building appropriate to the town, which was then enjoying the status of being a fashionable place to live.

MARKET PLACE c1955
To the left of the Town Hall is the local branch of the National Provincial Bank, while to the right The Central Pharmacy is still a chemists, but under the name of Cherrington. What had once been Johnson's Toy & Fancy Bazaar is now a branch of Curry's.

THE TOWN HALL c1955 N12005

MARKET PLACE c1955 N12009V

MARKET PLACE 1890 24655

A bustling market day. On the right are the Saracen's Head and the Clinton Arms Hotel, which once boasted stabling facilities for no less than ninety horses. In the background are the premises of W A Gilbey, purveyors of Gilbey's invalid port, and the tea, coffee, and spice warehouse of J M Walker. Gilbey's later became Knight's drapers store, and Gilbey moved next door into Walker's old establishment.

A SWIFT

MARKET PLACE 1923 74605
Formerly the Kingston Arms coaching inn, the Clinton Arms has connections with Lord Byron, who stayed here whilst his first book of poems, 'Fugitive Pieces', was being printed at the local firm of S & J Ridge. The future prime minister William Gladstone gave his first ever public speech in his political career from one of the inn's windows. Gladstone was a nominee of the Duke of Newcastle, who effectively chose Newark's members of parliament. In May 1831 Thomas Wilde managed to upset the duke by winning a seat; the duke retaliated by evicting those of his tenants who had voted for Wilde.

Ye Olde White Hart c1955 N12006

Ye Olde White Hart c1955
Dating from the 14th century, the White Hart is one of the oldest surviving examples of domestic architecture in the East Midlands. It is situated in the south-east corner of the Market Place.

The White Hart Yard c1955
When the inn was built in the 14th century Newark was one of the most important market towns in the East Midlands, and about the same size as Nottingham. During the reign of Edward III, Flemish weavers and merchants settled in Newark, which was an export centre for the wool trade with the Low Countries.

The White Hart Yard c1955 N12003

MARKET PLACE 1923 74606
Around a hundred years before this picture was taken, the cobblestones of Newark Market Place would have echoed to the clatter of stagecoaches and carriers' waggons. The early 1830s were the boom years for the stagecoach industry, with around 3500 scheduled runs taking to the roads every day. Thirty coaches a day made scheduled stops at Newark, with additional services operated by local carriers within a 10-15 mile radius of the town.

Market Place c1965 N12062
This view was taken from the spire of St Mary's, and what a quiet day it is. In previous centuries Market Places were often where pillories were sited, and though there are few surviving references to their use in 17th-century Nottinghamshire, they are known to have existed at Nottingham, Newark, Bingham and Mansfield. There was also a whipping post at Newark.

Market Place 1900 45105
This photograph gives a clear view of the premises along this side of the Market Place, with a superb display at the Star Tea Co (the expert tasters and blenders). Another largish outlet selling teas and coffees was Porters; their shop can be seen at right in the next photograph.

EASTMANS LIMITED
EASTMANS SHOPS EVERYWHERE
THE CENTRAL PRINTING WORKS
STENNETT
DENNIS

RIEND & Co
W. SMITH
PORTER
T
PORTER
TEAS

THE POST OFFICE 1908 59944

THE POST OFFICE 1908

In Victorian and Edwardian times the post offices was considered an essential service for the public good. In large cities the main post offices had long opening hours, often from 8.00am to 10.00pm, and offered a wide range of postal and telegraphic services. Smaller offices such as Newark's were still important, and ensured that deliveries were made even on Christmas Day. The post office was designed by Newark architects Saunders & Saunders and opened in 1908.

GENERAL VIEW c1965

In this view from the top of St Mary's tower, the castle ruins can be seen in the centre background. Following Newark's surrender, the Parliamentarians smashed the bowl of the 15th-century font in St Mary's; it was eventually replaced around 1660. This act of restoration has resulted in the 15th-century saints having mid 17th-century heads.

GENERAL VIEW c1965 N12060

FROM THE CHURCH TOWER 1923 74604
The church is worth a visit, if only for its early 16th-century black rood screen, the only surviving example of the work of Thomas Drawsword. The reredos looks as though it might date from the 14th century, but is in fact by Sir Ninian Comper, whose other work in Nottinghamshire includes a rood screen at St Mary's, Egmanton (1896), and a statue of the Virgin at St Mary the Virgin, Clumber Park.

THE PARISH CHURCH c1875 7807
The Chancel of St Mary Magdalen. Rebuilding of the original church began around the year 1230, when a new west tower was added. Over the following two hundred years or so St Mary's was transformed from a rather plain building into one of the finest parish churches in England.

THE PARISH CHURCH c1955 N12010
St Mary's is well known for the large number of chantries endowed by Newark's wealthier inhabitants. Many wealthy merchants, such as Thomas Meering, made sure that there was provision in their wills to enable a priest to say a Mass every day for the good of their souls. For its size, St Mary's had more chantries than most parish churches, an indication of just how prosperous the town was between the 13th and 16th centuries.

QUEEN'S GATE MEWS c1965 N12102
When the half-timbered Queen's Head Inn was being built in Newark in the 16th century, the largest town in the East Midlands was probably Leicester, closely followed by Nottingham. These two towns had populations of between 3000 and 3300 people. Derby and Lincoln were hovering around the 2000 - 2200 mark. Newark had by now lost ground, and its population was around 1500.

Chain Lane c1965 N12091

Many visitors enjoy exploring the town's courtyards and narrow alleyways, most of which were probably laid out in Anglo-Saxon or medieval times. As with Derby, Nottingham, Mansfield and Retford, some Newark street names hark back to the Danelaw. The Danish word for road is 'gata', which appears in its anglicised form at Newark in Appleton Gate, Balderton Gate and Barnby Gate.

BARNBY GATE 1904 51742

On the right is the Wesleyan Chapel. John Wesley visited Newark on six occasions between 1743 and 1788. After his last visit he described the Newark Methodists as 'a numerous, serious and deeply attentive congregation'. The chapel, capable of holding 1400 people, opened in July 1846 at a total cost including land of £5200. The Methodist New Connection opened their chapel in October 1848.

BARNBY GATE C1955 N12027

On the right is the Rutland Arms, a commercial hotel. Commercial hotels evolved to offer businessmen, company representatives and travellers (salesmen) comfortable and affordable accommodation. In pre-world war two days, most travellers toured their patch by train and tram, hiring a barrow-boy if necessary to trundle their wares between calls. One story tells of the landlord of a commercial hotel: finding that a traveller had died in his sleep, he telegraphed to the company concerned. They telegraphed back 'SORRY TO HEAR ABOUT THE DEATH STOP. PLEASE SEND BACK SAMPLES STOP'.

THE GRAMMAR SCHOOL 1909 61806

The Grammar School was founded in 1238. One of its famous benefactors was Dr Thomas Magnus (d 1550), who after going to Oxford became one of Henry VIII's chaplains, and in 1520 was appointed Canon of Windsor. Thomas was also entrusted with diplomatic missions to France and Scotland, and became wealthy enough to bequeath his old school 2000 acres plus the rents from a number of houses.

The Grammar School 1909 61805
According to the terms of Dr Magnus's will the Trustees were to appoint 'two secular honest priests, one to have sufficient cunning and learning to teach grammar, and the other to have cunning and learning to teach plain song, descant, and playing on the organs'.

The School of Science and Art 1904 51744
At least the students here did not suffer the timetable imposed upon the Grammar School by Dr Magnus. He recommended that the school day should begin at 6.00am and go on till 9.00am, when breakfast was to be taken. Lessons were to resume at ten and go on till mid-day, when dinner was to be served. The afternoon session was to start at either one or half-past and continue until 6.00pm. The good doctor did say that scholars were to be allowed some afternoons off, but only so that they could attend Mass.

MAGNUS STREET 1908 59943

This street is named after Dr Thomas Magnus. There are a couple of traditional stories relating to Thomas's childhood. One is that he was found abandoned in the parish church by some Yorkshire clothiers who were passing through the town on their way home. They agreed to provide for the baby and had him baptised Thomas, giving him the surname of Amangus, the name supposedly meaning 'to be maintained by us'. The second tradition is that Thomas was the son of a local inn keeper who had fallen on hard times. The Yorkshire clothiers are said to have concluded that given the right opportunity, young Thomas had potential for great things, so they offered to take him with them and provide for his education and welfare. Whatever the truth of the stories, Thomas certainly went on to do great things.

KIRKGATE 1900 45106

During the 17th century there were many indictments for disturbing divine services; some of the persons charged were themselves clergymen. In January 1618 Lucas Mason and Christopher Martley, clerks, both of Newark, were indicted along with a labourer from Hockerton for 'riotously entering a church'; while Nathaniel Wooley, clerk, of Hockerton, was also up before the justices, indicted for 'disturbing clergymen during prayers'.

THE ROMAN CATHOLIC CHURCH 1908 59945

THE ROMAN CATHOLIC CHURCH 1908
In 1827, opinion in the town on Catholic emancipation seems to have been divided. There were appeals in the local press for it to be granted, yet a petition against emancipation on the grounds that it would undermine the Protestant Establishment was sent to London signed by 1100 inhabitants, including the mayor.

ST LEONARD'S CHURCH 1890
Built at a total cost of £4000 including land, St Leonard's Church opened in 1873, the same year that St Leonard's district was created. Built of stone in the early decorated style, the church could accommodate 600 people.

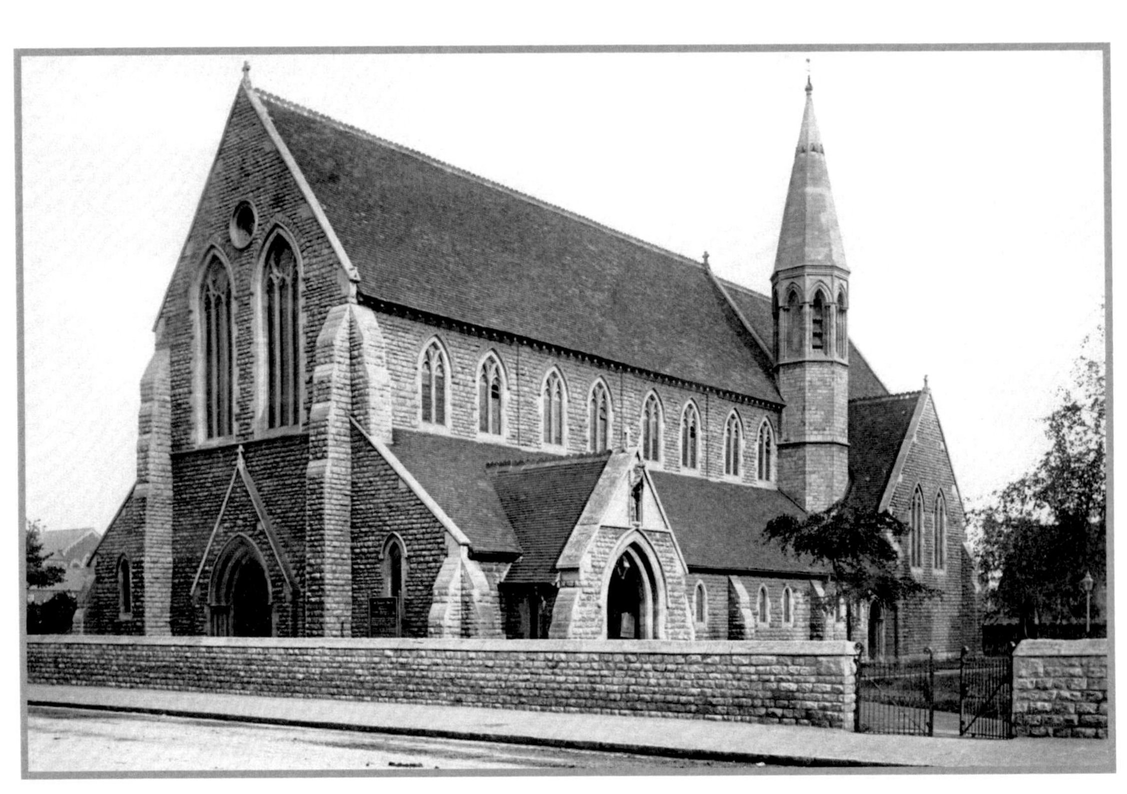

ST LEONARD'S CHURCH 1890 24674

London Road 1909 61798
London Road at this time appears to be reasonably well maintained, though there was a time when roads were anything but. Parishes were responsible for repairs to roads within their territory, but many did little or nothing to meet their obligations. In the 17th century, the only stretch of the Fosse Way known to have been maintained was that between East Stoke and Newark.

THE HOSPITAL AND LONDON ROAD 1904 51743

The hospital and dispensary were two of a large number of 19th-century developments carried out for the benefit of the inhabitants. Others included the provision of libraries, new schools, such as the Christ Church Boys' School of 1850 and the Girls' School of 1856, and a spate of chapel building in the 1860s and 70s.

THE INFIRMARY 1909 61807

This photograph was taken in the days when only the fit went to hospital; you needed to be for matron's rounds. Patients lay in their bed, not on it, legs together, arms out of the blankets pressed firmly to the side of the body. Those allowed to sit upright did so, but with their arms folded. Patients were not allowed to ask questions, and were to speak only if requested to do so.

The Cemetery 1904 51746

This is not Newark's only cemetery. In 1724 William Stukeley recorded that workmen digging in Millgate had unearthed four cremation urns, the first real indication that an ancient burial site existed near the town. It was not until the 1960s that a major archaeological dig was mounted; the site proved to be Anglo-Saxon, dating from the early 5th to the early 7th centuries.

Cemetery Avenue 1904 51745

There exists at least one account that states that the plague reached Newark in the summer of 1665, said to have been brought to the town in contaminated patterns of woollen cloths delivered to a draper in the market place. Burials were forbidden within the town, and a plague pit was opened at the southern end of Millgate near the bridge over the Devon. Writing in 1879, Cornelius Brown said that he could find no evidence to support the plague story; church records showed no unusual increase in the number of recorded deaths, and that the inhabitants of Newark were in fact sending financial aid to infected areas.

FOUNTAIN GARDEN c1955 N12024

As this view was taken for possible publication as a postcard, our cameraman adhered to company policy by making sure there were no people in the picture. This was purely commercial: changing fashions date pictures quickly, and Frith wanted the postcard in circulation for as long as possible.

FRIARY GARDENS c1955 N12051

Rustic benches and rose arches form the subject of this picture, and would have made an attractive postcard.

The Swimming Pool c1955 N12016

The Beaumond Cross 1904 51739

The Swimming Pool c1955

Was the East Midland's climate ever that good? Open-air swimming pools are probably the direct descendants of the sea-bathing craze that swept the country during the 19th century. Many towns had open-air pools, though few now survive. They went out of fashion; many were closed on health and safety grounds.

The Beaumond Cross 1904

The Beaumond Cross at the end of Carter Gate on the southern approach to the town is thought to date from the 14th or 15th centuries, and might be a wayside praying cross. Here travellers either gave thanks for their safe arrival in Newark, or sought Christ's protection before setting off on a journey.

THE BOATHOUSE 1909 61801
In earlier times both the Trent and the Devon were actively fished, sometimes illegally. In July 1613 'a fisher of Newark and a ffowler of ffarndon' were indicted for obstructing the Devon, probably with illegal nets. On the right is Jobson's Boathouse. Jobson's business included boat building and boat hire.

DEVON BRIDGE 1909 61802
The Devon is in reality a branch of the Trent, but it played a vital role in Newark's commercial success. By the mid 7th century around 16,000 tonnes of coal were being brought annually to Newark by river, where they were exchanged for malt and corn. In 1742 the town sponsored a Bill to change the course of the Trent, which would have enhanced its position as an inland port. Needless to say, Nottingham considered that such a proposal would harm its trade and opposed the Bill. In 1772 Newark was successful, and was authorised to improve the navigation of the river.

On the Trent 1906 56505
Rising as it does in the hills on the Staffordshire and Cheshire borders, the Trent in 1885 was estimated at being about 150 miles in length with a drainage area of 4050 square miles, of which 2900 were above Nottingham. Only the Thames and the Severn had larger watersheds.

The Old Mill 1906 56503
Newark's position on the Great North Road and the River Trent attracted industry including flour milling, maltings, brewing, an iron works, leather working, and even a glue factory. Between 1801 and 1901 the population rocketed from 6000 to 15,000, but even so it had long lost the fight against its great commercial rival Nottingham.

THE RIVER c1965 N12078
Warehouses and industry flourish along the banks of the river. In 1968, when work was underway on a new Devon Bridge, timber piles and some stonework were discovered on the river bed. The find was enough to convince the experts that the Roman crossing point had been located, though there is still some debate as to the original course of the Roman road.

THE RIVER DEVON c1965 N12059
On the way into Newark from Farndon the navigation passes a number of old maltings and a large Trent Navigation Co warehouse, which can be seen in this picture in the left background.

Balderton, The Village 1909 61813
In 1909 Balderton was a farming parish adjacent to Newark. In the late 17th century the local freeholders and copyholders were happy to accept enclosure of their open-field system, and came to a private arrangement with Robert Williams of Balderton manor. Adopting enclosure meant that sheep and cattle could be kept away from crops.

BALDERTON, THE VILLAGE 1909 61814
The builder of Syerston Hall, William Fillingham, has a connection with Balderton in that his ancestors were farmers there. Though William was himself a farmer, he was also a land surveyor, property developer and investor in canals. He obtained Syerston in 1792 when he bought 500 acres from Lewis Fytche for £12,375. William died before Syerston Hall was finished; it was completed by his son, George.

BALDERTON, THE WESLEYAN CHURCH 1909 61816
It was after they had founded the Holy Club at Oxford in 1729 that John and Charles Wesley began their evangelical missionary work with a trip to Georgia. It was there that the basic principles of what would become the Methodist movement were first established. John returned home to spread the word. He visited nearby Newark six times between 1743 and 1788.

FARNDON FERRY 1923 74627
There has been a ferry at Farndon for centuries; these days the village offers river users extensive facilities, including a large marina created out of some old gravel pits.

KELHAM HALL 1890 24696
Kelham Hall was designed by Sir Gilbert Scott to replace an earlier structure destroyed by fire in the late 1850s. It was at the original hall that King Charles I is said to have finally surrendered to the Scots in 1645. The King's arrival at Newark had taken the Scots by surprise, but they immediately sounded Parliament out with a view to eventually selling his majesty to the English.

KELHAM HALL BRIDGE 1904 51749
Situated between the Hall and the village, Kelham Bridge's one claim to fame is that it was rammed and split in two by a small iceberg that floated down the Trent during the winter of 1854-55.

Rolleston, The Church c1955 R325004
Situated between Southwell and Newark, Rolleston once had a moated manor house held by the Neville family. Rolleston Junction was where the Midland Railway lines from Mansfield to Newark via Southwell, and Nottingham Midland to Newark met.

Southwell, The Minster 1895 35558
Southwell is a Norman church built on the site of a Saxon minster founded in AD956 on land given to Oscytel, Archbishop of York, by King Eadwig. All that remains of the Saxon building is a carved doorhead in the north transept and some paving in the south transept. This view shows the west towers, one either side of the large Perpendicular window, with the low central tower bringing up the rear.

SOUTHWELL, KING STREET 1920 69472
King Street is the location of the former market place, which was built over many years ago. Also along here is the timber-framed Saracen's Head. In 1646 it was known as the King's Arms; it was here that Charles I spent his last hours of freedom before surrendering to the Scots.

ADMIRAL RODNEY HOTEL
ADMIRA
FAMILY
WORKSOP
F.C.HEALD.

WINTHORPE BRIDGE 1923 74624

WINTHORPE, THE CHURCH 1890 24687

WINTHORPE BRIDGE 1923

In the late 18th century a ferry operated between Muskham and Newark, but the owners soon gained a reputation for being greedy when the river was in flood; there is one instance of them charging five guineas to ferry a carriage and its passengers. In 1770 a bridge cum elevated road was constructed, which put paid to the ferry.

WINTHORPE
The Church 1890

In this picture the ancient village church looks brand new; it was. The Reverend Edward Hadley had All Saints completely rebuilt between 1886 and 1888, and paid for it himself.

WINTHORPE, THE VILLAGE 1909 61809
The world seems to have passed Winthorpe by. The A1 is between it and Newark, so the village is free from through traffic. The Midland Railway line between Newark and Lincoln skirted the northern edge of the village. Up to the end of 1847 Winthorpe appeared in the Midland timetable, but it appears that no train ever stopped there.

HOLME, THE CHURCH 1909 61810
Holme is a hamlet on the east bank of the Trent slightly north of Winthorpe. The church was rebuilt in 1485 by John Barton of Calais. It is distinctive in that its porch, with its upper room and flanking round tower, would look more at home on a fortified manor house. It is said that during the Great Plague one of the villagers took refuge inside the church. Eventually, having run out of food, she came out. All were dead except for just one man.

Index

FRITH PRODUCTS & SERVICES

Francis Frith would doubtless be pleased to know that the pioneering publishing venture he started in 1860 still continues today. Over a hundred and forty years later, The Francis Frith Collection continues in the same innovative tradition and is now one of the foremost publishers of vintage photographs in the world. Some of the current activities include:

INTERIOR DECORATION

Today Frith's photographs can be seen framed and as giant wall murals in thousands of pubs, restaurants, hotels, banks, retail stores and other public buildings throughout the country. In every case they enhance the unique local atmosphere of the places they depict and provide reminders of gentler days in an increasingly busy and frenetic world.

PRODUCT PROMOTIONS

Frith products are used by many major companies to promote the sales of their own products or to reinforce their own history and heritage. Frith promotions have been used by Hovis bread, Courage beers, Scots Porage Oats, Colman's mustard, Cadbury's foods, Mellow Birds coffee, Dunhill pipe tobacco, Guinness, and Bulmer's Cider.

GENEALOGY AND FAMILY HISTORY

As the interest in family history and roots grows world-wide, more and more people are turning to Frith's photographs of Great Britain for images of the towns, villages and streets where their ancestors lived; and, of course, photographs of the churches and chapels where their ancestors were christened, married and buried are an essential part of every genealogy tree and family album.

FRITH PRODUCTS

All Frith photographs are available Framed or just as Mounted Prints and unmounted versions. These may be ordered from the address below. Other products available are - Calendars, Jigsaws, Canvas Prints, Mugs, Tea Towels, Tableware and local and prestige books.

THE INTERNET

Over several hundred thousand Frith photographs can be viewed and purchased on the internet through the Frith websites!

For more detailed information on Frith products, look at www.francisfrith.com

See the complete list of Frith Books at: www.francisfrith.com

This web site is regularly updated with the latest list of publications from The Francis Frith Collection. If you wish to buy books relating to another part of the country that your local bookshop does not stock, you may purchase on-line.

For further information, trade, or author enquiries please contact us at the address below:

The Francis Frith Collection, Unit 19 Kingsmead Business Park, Gillingham, Dorset SP8 5FB.

Tel: +44 (0)1722 716 376 Email: sales@francisfrith.co.uk

See Frith products on the internet at www.francisfrith.com

FREE PRINT OF YOUR CHOICE

CHOOSE A PHOTOGRAPH FROM THIS BOOK

+ POSTAGE

Mounted Print
Overall size 14 x 11 inches (355 x 280mm)

TO RECEIVE YOUR FREE PRINT

Choose any Frith photograph in this book

Simply complete the Voucher opposite and return it with your payment (to cover postage and handling) and we will print the photograph of your choice in SEPIA (size 11 x 8 inches) and supply it in a cream mount ready to frame (overall size 14 x 11 inches).

Order additional Mounted Prints at HALF PRICE - £19.00 each (normally £38.00)

If you would like to order more Frith prints from this book, possibly as gifts for friends and family, you can buy them at half price (with no additional postage costs).

Have your Mounted Prints framed

For an extra £20.00 per print you can have your mounted print(s) framed in an elegant polished wood and gilt moulding, overall size 16 x 13 inches (no additional postage required).

IMPORTANT!

❶ Please note: aerial photographs and photographs with a reference number starting with a "Z" are not Frith photographs and cannot be supplied under this offer.

❷ Offer valid for delivery to one UK address only.

❸ These special prices are only available if you use this form to order. You must use the ORIGINAL VOUCHER on this page (no copies permitted). We can only despatch to one UK address.

❹ This offer cannot be combined with any other offer.

As a customer your name & address will be stored by Frith but not sold or rented to third parties. Your data will be used for the purpose of this promotion only.

Send completed Voucher form to:

The Francis Frith Collection,
19 Kingsmead Business Park, Gillingham,
Dorset SP8 5FB

Voucher *for FREE and Reduced Price Frith Prints*

Please do not photocopy this voucher. Only the original is valid, so please fill it in, cut it out and return it to us with your order.

Picture ref no	Page no	Qty	Mounted @ £19.00	Framed + £20.00	Total Cost £
		1	Free of charge*	£	£
			£19.00	£	£
			£19.00	£	£
			£19.00	£	£
			£19.00	£	£
			£19.00	£	£
			* Post & handling		£3.80
			Total Order Cost		£

Please allow 28 days for delivery.
Offer available to one UK address only

Title of this book ....

I enclose a cheque/postal order for £ ....
made payable to 'The Francis Frith Collection'

OR please debit my Mastercard / Visa / Maestro card, details below

Card Number:

Issue No (Maestro only): Valid from (Maestro):

Card Security Number: Expires:

Signature:

Name Mr/Mrs/Ms ....

Address ....

....

....

.... Postcode ....

Daytime Tel No ....

Email ....

Valid to 31/12/20

Free Print - see overleaf

Can you help us with information about any of the Frith photographs in this book?

We are gradually compiling an historical record for each of the photographs in the Frith archive. It is always fascinating to find out the names of the people shown in the pictures, as well as insights into the shops, buildings and other features depicted.

If you recognize anyone in the photographs in this book, or if you have information not already included in the author's caption, do let us know. We would love to hear from you, and will try to publish it in future books or articles.

An Invitation from The Francis Frith Collection to Share Your Memories

The 'Share Your Memories' feature of our website allows members of the public to add personal memories relating to the places featured in our photographs, or comment on others already added. Seeing a place from your past can rekindle forgotten or long held memories. Why not visit the website, find photographs of places you know well and add YOUR story for others to read and enjoy? We would love to hear from you!

www.francisfrith.com/memories

Our production team

Frith books are produced by a small dedicated team at offices near Salisbury. Most have worked with the Frith Collection for many years. All have in common one quality: they have a passion for the Frith Collection.

Frith Books and Gifts

We have a wide range of books and gifts available on our website utilising our photographic archive, many of which can be individually personalised.

www.francisfrith.com

FF026340